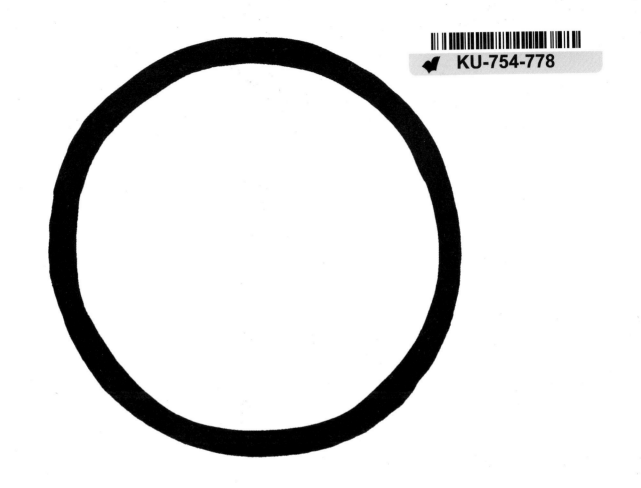

Kruh

A circle

Jedna čára. Mnoho čar.

One line. Many lines.

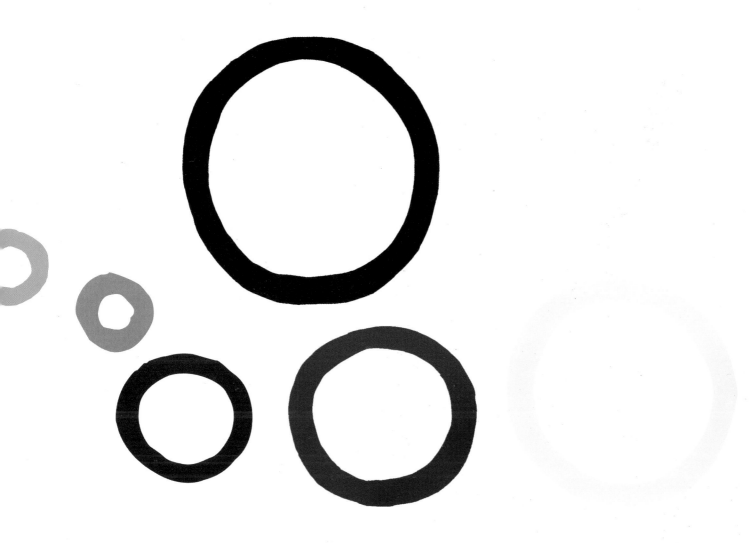

Jeden kruh. Mnoho kruhů.

One circle. Many circles.

Čára se klikatí.

Line runs.

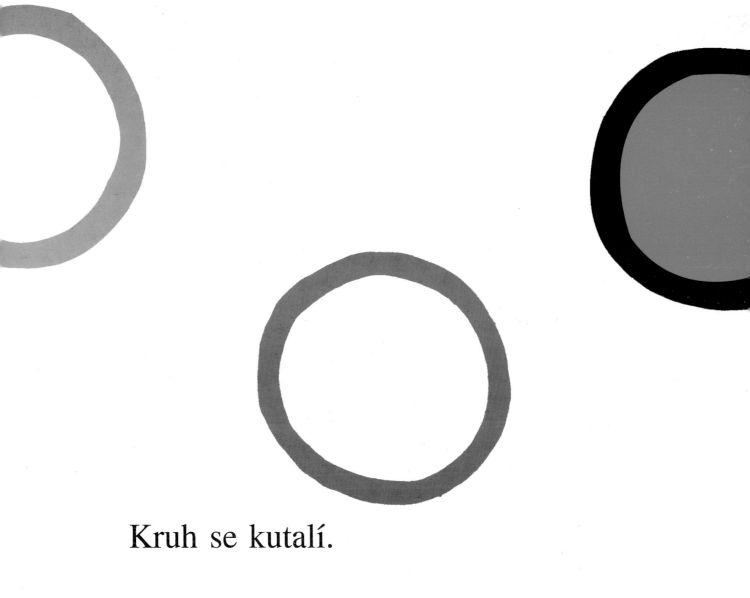

Kruh se kutalí.

Circle rolls.

Čára a kruh se setkávají.

Line and circle meet.

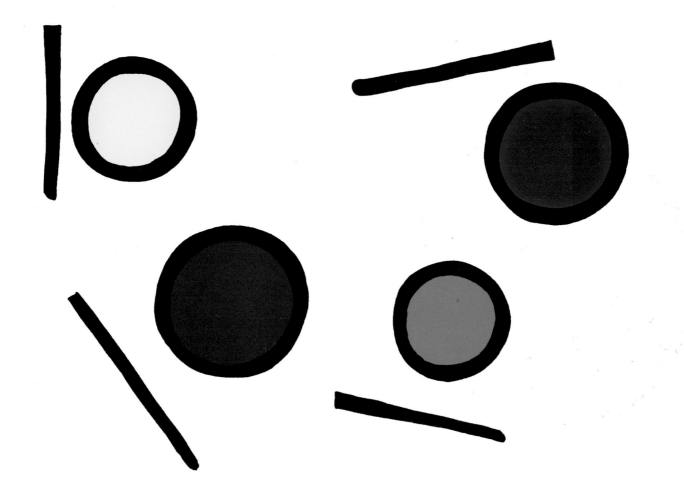

Tady, tam. Tady a tam. Všude.

Here, there. Here and there. Everywhere.

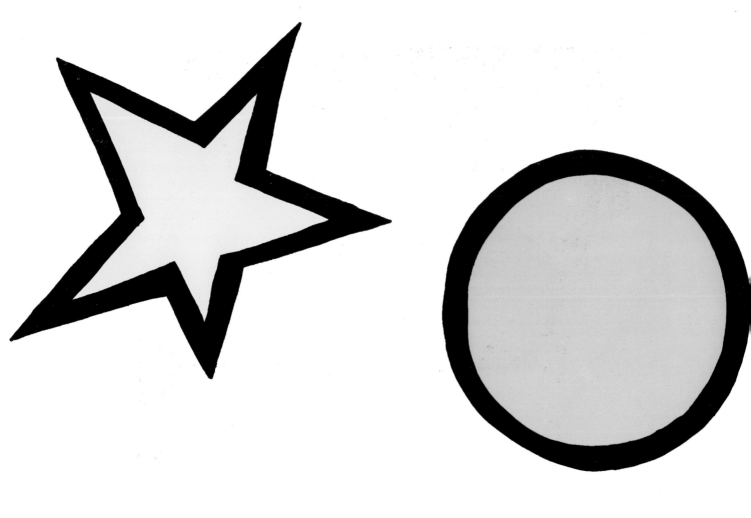

Čára je hvězda. Kruh je měsíc.

Line is a star. Circle is the moon.

Čára je stůl. Kruh je talíř.

Line is a table. Circle is the plate.

Brzy se stávají přáteli.
Dohromady mohou dělat mnoho věcí.

Soon they are friends.
Together they make many things.

Sun   Slunce

Flower

Květinu

Fruit   Ovoce

Wheel   Kolo

Tree

Strom

Bird   Ptáčka

Face   Obličej

Fish

Rybičku

Výborně se u toho bavily.

They had lots of fun.

Vy také?

Did you?

Other dual language books for 3 - 5 year olds from Mantra

Alfie's Angels by Henriette Barkow & Sarah Garson
Brown Bear, Brown Bear, What Do You See? by Bill Martin & Eric Carle
Goldilocks by Kate Clynes & Louise Daykin
Floppy by Guido Van Genechten
Floppy in the Dark by Guido Van Genechten
Handa's Hens by Eileen Brown
Handa's Surprise by Eileen Brown
Head Shoulders Knees and Toes byAnnie Kubler
Mei Ling's Hiccups by David Mills & Derek Brazell
Paddington Bear All Day by Michael Bond
Paddington Goes to Market by Michael Bond
Sam's First Day by David Mills & Lizzie Finlay
Sleepyhead by Nicola Smee
Splash by Flora McDonnell
The Swirling Hijaab by Na'ima bint Robert & Nilesh Mistry
The Very Hungry Caterpillar by Eric Carle
Walking through the Jungle by Debbie Harter
What shall we do with the Boo Hoo Baby? by Cressida Cowell & Ingrid Godon
We're Going on a Bear Hunt by Michael Rosen & Helen Oxenbury

Concept and Author: Radhika Menon

Copyright © 1996 Tulika Dual language text copyright © 2003 Mantra
First published in India by Tulika Publishers, Chennai, India, 1996
All rights reserved
British Library Cataloguing in Publication Data: a catalogue record
for this book is available from the British Library.
Printed by Anjan International Media, Chennai, India

Mantra Lingua

5 Alexandra Grove, London N12 8NU, UK
www.mantralingua.com